James Abercorn

Report of the Proceedings at the Great Aggregate Meeting

of the Irish Landlords

1882

James Abercorn

Report of the Proceedings at the Great Aggregate Meeting of the Irish Landlords
1882

ISBN/EAN: 9783337124915

Printed in Europe, USA, Canada, Australia, Japan

Cover: Foto ©Suzi / pixelio.de

More available books at **www.hansebooks.com**

REPORT OF THE PROCEEDINGS

AT THE

GREAT AGGREGATE MEETING

OF

THE IRISH LANDLORDS,

HELD IN DUBLIN,

ON TUESDAY, 3rd JANUARY, 1882.

HIS GRACE THE DUKE OF ABERCORN
IN THE CHAIR.

DUBLIN:

HODGES, FIGGIS, & CO, 104, GRAFTON-STREET,
PUBLISHERS TO THE UNIVERSITY.

1882.

REPORT OF PROCEEDINGS,

&c. &c.

His Grace the DUKE of ABERCORN,

in taking the chair, said:—

My Lords and Gentlemen, I thank you most heartily for your kind welcome, and I accept with pleasure the honour you have done me in proposing me as your chairman over this great and important meeting. I will open the proceedings by calling on Colonel Tottenham to read the letters that have been received from noblemen and gentlemen sympathizing with and approving of the objects of our meeting.

Lieut.-Col. LOFTUS A. TOTTENHAM, M.P.

Your Grace, my Lords and Gentlemen,—A large number of letters have been received from all parts of the country, in every case expressing favourable opinions as to the objects of this meeting. It would not do for us to take up the time of the meeting by reading all the letters, but we have selected a few as being representative opinions, which, with the permission of the meeting, I will read to you. The first is from the EARL OF MEATH. It is:—

"My dear Lord,—Although considerably recovered from my late illness, I am not yet strong enough to participate in public business, and I am therefore compelled with great regret to absent myself from the great meeting of Irish landowners, to which I wish to give my most cordial support. I consider it a duty incumbent on every landowner to raise an indignant protest against the partial and unjust decisions given by the Sub-Commissions in their administration of the Land Act, and this censure I am convinced will be pronounced with no uncertain voice by the meeting to-morrow. Though personally unable to assist, my best wishes are with the opinions and objects the meeting has met to proclaim.—Believe me, yours truly,

"MEATH."

The next letter is one from EARL FITZWILLIAM, who writes :—

"I fear I cannot be in Dublin on the 3rd of January. This is a matter of regret to me. The Land Act must, of course, be now accepted by all loyal men, but we cannot press too strongly upon the Government the absolute necessity of appointing as Sub-Commissioners men whose character for impartiality and justice has already earned the confidence and respect of the community at large. A great portion of the country is already terribly demoralized, and I cannot but fear that the present action of the Government is leading to still more deplorable results."

The third is from the EARL OF PEMBROKE :—

"MY LORD DUKE,—I very much regret not being able to attend the meeting in Dublin on Tuesday. Perhaps you would kindly mention this. I should like my name to appear as one who, at least, wanted to be there."

The next is from LORD HOWTH, who says :—

"In reply to the circular forwarded me, I regret being unable to attend the meeting of Irish landowners on January 3rd, which it is proposed to hold, for the purpose of taking into consideration the administration of the Land Act. Allow me to add I support the object of the meeting."

Mr. JOHN MULHOLLAND, the Member for Downpatrick—who, I may mention, was to have proposed or seconded one of the resolutions, but who has, unfortunately, been detained by a very serious accident that has occurred to members of his family—writes :—

"I regret exceedingly that I am unavoidably prevented from attending the meeting of landowners to-morrow. Having been one of those who supported the Land Act, I had intended to explain that my support was given on the faith of the assurance of Mr. Gladstone that the intention of the Fair Rent

Clause was to meet those cases (comparatively few and exceptional) where rent had been arbitrarily increased, and that it was not the intention to disturb the existing standard, practically well understood. The Sub-Commissioners have been reducing rents generally; the 'principle' upon which they are doing so has not been disclosed, but it is certainly not the principle of Mr. Gladstone. If a new standard of valuation is to be really introduced, there can be no doubt that it can only be done by a general re-valuation of Ireland upon a uniform principle, conducted by properly trained and qualified valuers. As a 'valuation,' the present system is a farce."

A letter has also been received approving generally of the objects of the meeting, and condemning very strongly certain portions of the Land Act, from Sir George Bowyer, who writes in his capacity as an old Irish member.

THE CHAIRMAN,

who was received with loud and prolonged applause, said :—

My Lords and Gentlemen I believe the meeting will concur with me when I say that our object is not to condemn or to criticise the Land Act itself; which, whatever may be our opinions of its injustice or its honesty, we still accept as a legislative enactment. Neither do we wish to enter into any political questions. But our object is to condemn and criticize the mode in which the Land Act has been administered by the local Sub-Commissioners; and I believe the meeting will concur with me when I say that we do so in no spirit of hostility to the tenants who may have thought it their interest to take advantage of the Act. My Lords and Gentlemen, that Act was passed through Parliament, after much opposition and many misgivings, on the repeated and reiterated assurance and promise that it should be administered with justice and impartiality. The Prime Minister on more than one occasion expressed his opinion that as a rule the landlords of Ireland had dealt justly and fairly with their tenants. The same impression was conceived by the Bessborough Commission, which could not be accused of a leaning too favourable towards the landlords, and from whose report a great part of the Land Act was evolved.

Mr. Gladstone, on introducing the measure, speaking of the Land League proposal, which then was to pay only Griffith's valuation, said:—"I am bound to say that it passes my ability to distinguish these proposals from public plunder." The Irish landlords have stood their trial, and they have, as a rule, been acquitted. On the second reading he said—The proposed principle of confiscation would be a disgrace to the Minister who discussed it, and to the Parliament which tolerated it for a single moment. On the 7th of October, Mr. Gladstone, speaking of the Land League, said—"Mr Parnell told the people of Ireland not to pay the rents which they had covenanted to pay; that, whether they were able or unable, they were under no obligation to pay those rents, but that they might pay rents according to the view set down in Griffith's valuation—a valuation (In Mr. Gladstone's words) much below the value in by far the greater number of cases, and framed for a different purpose."

Mr. Bright, on the second reading of the Bill, said: "My view of the clause (that relating to the fixing of rents) is, that in reality the rents in Ireland, for the most part, in nine cases out of ten, will be fixed very much as they are now." My Lords and Gentlemen, these are some of the specious and persuasive arguments that were used in passing the Land Act. How have these promises been kept—how have these assurances been verified? The Land Act has been passed, the country has been flooded with Sub-Commissioners, and we have seen wholesale reductions in every case. Twenty, thirty, forty, and sometimes fifty per cent. reductions have been almost universally made, except, I believe, in half-a-dozen cases, one of which is the notable case of half-a-crown.

I may take this opportunity of saying that I have personally no cause of complaint with the Sub-Commissioners, for any cases that I may have have not yet come into court. But we see from all parts of Ireland that wholesale reductions have been the order of the day. Whether the Sub-Commissioners have had instructions for a general reduction, whether they have acted *propria motu* to reduce the rents of the tenants, in order to show them the advantages to be derived from their judgments, or whether, as Professor Baldwin, dressed in a little brief authority, has stated, the lines of their decisions are to be given or determined before they have heard any cases at all, these lines presumably being a general reduction. Whatever may be the cause, the fact is patent that reductions have been almost universal, without any fixed rule, without any standard, or without any rule admitted for valuation; no valuator of known or experienced reputation having been employed by the Sub-Commissioners, while valuators of the highest professional reputation, if they gave their evidence in a way not favourable to the tenant, were treated with complete indifference. Many of the Sub-Commissioners have had little or no practice in the valuation of land; but, notwithstanding this, they undertake to do in two or three hours what professional valuators of the highest reputation would scarcely undertake to do in as many days. And it is on valuations made in this off-hand and haphazard manner—valuations made in the dead of winter, with the ground partially covered with snow, the land saturated with moisture, and the crops blackened and burned with frost—it is on valuations made in this manner rents have been reduced twenty, thirty, and more than that per cent. I am aware of a case in which the Sub-Commissioners went to value farms, containing in the aggregate more than 1100 acres, including grazing. They went in the short days of December thirty statute miles out, they came back thirty statute miles, they arrived on the ground at a quarter past two o'clock in the afternoon, they left the ground at a quarter past four o'clock in the afternoon. Upon this cursory and haphazard bird's-eye view reductions are made of twenty-five per cent. upon the rental, and twenty per cent. below the Government valuation, which had been very nearly the same as the original rents.

Now, gentlemen, it must be admitted that the Sub-Commissioners are conscientious—we must give them credit for that —in not sparing either their labour or their time; but valuations made in that haphazard way are nothing but a preposterous farce. They are nothing but a farce, and they would be nothing but a farce did they not entail ruin upon the smaller landlords, and great distress and inconvenience upon the larger landlords of Ireland, whose whole fortune now depends upon valuations such as those made by the Sub-Commissioners in their administration of the Act. My lords and gentlemen, it is impossible to overrate the injustice and also the impolicy of such proceedings. There are, no doubt, many cases where rents have been fairly reduced, but in the cases of old established estates, where tenants for years have been prosperous and contented until the Land League agitation, there is no such excuse ; and I repeat that the Sub-Commissioners, in making these wholesale reductions for the sake of alluring tenants into the Land Court, and in the endeavour to pay off the Land League agitation by the sacrifice of the landlords' income—that the Sub-Commissioners have taken a most impolitic step as regards the Land Act itself, and one which will most materially impede its operations. My lords and gentlemen, I believe that if the reductions had been fair and reasonable, and given upon reasonable terms, the great body of the landlords of Ireland would not have offered much opposition to them. But the wholesale reductions that have been made have aroused and will arouse such a storm of appeals that the higher court will be blocked by them for months, perhaps years, without any satisfactory solution, and the Land Act, instead of settling the question between landlords and tenants, will, in the way it has been administered by the Sub-Commissioners, loosen all the ties that hitherto, and even now, remain between the proprietor and his tenants.

Gentlemen, it has been insisted upon in some of the Liberal and Radical papers that the landlords of Ireland have no right to complain of these reductions because the landlords of England and Scotland have also made reductions. I say this is altogether an untrue and false issue. The reductions which have been made in England are for the most part merely temporary abatements, made for a year or so in consequence of the bad seasons, and made by mutual agreement; but the reductions made in Ireland, which are much larger, have been made by an arbitrary and irresponsible body, and are not temporary abatements, but permanent reductions—reductions virtually in perpetuity for successive periods of fifteen years. On one ground alone it is impossible to compare the English and Scotch tenants with the case of the Irish, and that is, that the Irish tenant, under the Land Act of 1881, is able, if dissatisfied with his rent, to sell his farm for as much, or nearly as much, as his landlord could get for the fee-simple of it. I believe on these terms most English tenants would be too glad to change places with the Irish tenants; and, in order to make any comparison, you must suppose the English tenant rented at £500 a-year, you must suppose him selling his farm for £10,000, that is twenty years' purchase (a common tenant right in Ireland), and going off leaving his farm with £10,000 in his pocket. That is the comparison of the two.

My lords and gentlemen, the injustice and partiality displayed in some of the Commissioners' Courts will not be a matter of surprise, if we look to the constitution of those courts. The Sub-Commissioners are, no doubt, very respectable men, but they have been selected from a class antagonistic to the landlords, and favourable to the tenants. Many of them have been strong and firm tenant-right agitators; all of them—with few exceptions, three or four exceptions, I believe—are men of strong liberal and partisan opinions. I am aware of cases of appointments in which the only qualification was strong and violent tenant-right agitation and violent partisanship at the last general election. Gentlemen, it is into the hands of gentlemen of opinions such as these that the whole fortunes of the Irish landlords are now committed. I say, then, that in the appointment of these partisan officials the promises and the assurances which were made for passing the Land Act—promises and assurances which were given in a different direction, and by which the House of Lords was induced to grant its assent, and by which the majority of doubting and misgiving Liberals in the House of Commons were induced to support it—have been violated.

One of the promises on which Parliament was induced to sanction that measure was, that there should be three Head-Commissioners of undoubted ability and reputation appointed. Those gentlemen were named and approved by Parliament. What has been the result? The Land Act has been hitherto administered solely by a number of Sub-Commissioners. Unknown men selected at haphazard, who have acted quite independently of the Head-Commissioners, and who have acted without any rule, without any standard, without any explained principle except the principle of handing over a considerable portion of the landlord's income to the tenant. I maintain that these proceedings have no parallel in the judicial administration of the law hitherto in any part of the British Empire. We have then the right to claim that the false issues upon which the Land Act was passed, and upon which it has been hitherto administered, should be cleared away, and that henceforth it should be admistered with impartial justice, without any cravings for public applause in court, and with judicial moderation and equity towards the landlord as well as towards the tenant.

My lords and gentlemen, this great and important meeting, containing the representatives of the landowners in Ireland — men of all creeds and of all shades of politics, is an earnest that we will maintain and insist upon our right for impartial justice, and that we will not allow our fortunes and the birthrights of our children to be sacrificed in the vain attempt to propitiate and to appease a seditious and homicidal Land League.

It is now my duty as chairman to give way to the gentlemen who will speak to the several resolutions; but before I do so I wish to state that it is requested by the committee that any gentleman who may wish to speak, besides the movers and seconders of the resolutions, will be good enough to come to the platform.

The EARL of DARTREY,

on coming forward to move the first resolution, was cordially received. He said :—

My Lord Duke, my Lords and Gentlemen—I entirely agree in the observations with which the noble Duke commenced his speech, that it is no part of our business here to-day to discuss or criticise the Land Act of last session. That Act is now the law of the land, and I may say very much in the words of the resolution which I have now the honour of proposing for your adoption, that we, as loyal subjects, are prepared to adhere to its provisions. I am satisfied that every one of us will endeavour, to the best of our ability, to work it fairly and impartially, giving to our tenants in no grudging spirit the benefits to which they are now lawfully entitled. The manner, however, in which the Act has been administered is a totally different thing, and to protest against it is, I understand, the main object for which we are assembled here to-day.

The result of the two first months of the working of the Sub-Commissioners has been such as must fill with astonishment the mind of everyone who has followed them, and I am convinced that this astonishment must be shared not only by the great majority of the members of the Legislature who supported the Bill in Parliament, but also by Her Majesty's Ministers themselves. I would in particular refer to the Prime Minister, the Lord Chancellor, and the Lord Privy Seal, in all whose speeches recommending the measure to Parliament, they expressed most strongly, and as I believe most truly, the confident expectation of a totally different result. Parliament was induced to pass this Bill by strong representations that it would not diminish the value or disturb the foundations of property, and we were not told that in all cases rents, high or low, were to be dimished.

The Government most properly, before asking the final assent of Parliament to the Bill, thought it their duty to announce publicly the names of the three Commissioners who were to be intrusted with its working as a guarantee of the *bona fides* which should govern its administration, and also of the judicial impartiality with which justice ought to be meted out to landlord and tenant alike. As a further security for this, provision was made in the Bill for the employment of independent valuers in fixing rents. I observe, however, that this power has not been exercised except in one or two cases. I would also remark that when such precautions had been taken to satisfy public opinion, and to ensure that justice should be done, no one would have imagined that the most important part of the working of the Act would have been intrusted to a body of Sub-Commissioners, without any interference, for two months, on the part of the Government or the Head Commissioner. I forbear saying a word on the composition of the Sub-Commissions, as that is a subject not within the limit of my resolution, but I trust we shall have a good deal on that subject later on. I must again repeat, no one would have expected that the subordinate officials would have been sent on circuit throughout the country without, as far as the public knew, any specific rules or instructions being laid down for their guidance. But that has been frequently announced by the Sub-Commissioners themselves, who have boasted that they were entirely irresponsible and entirely uncontrolled ; and, therefore, I conclude that there can be no doubt about the matter. I would also remark that the extraordinary principles enunciated by some of the Commissioners, and the complete divergence of their practice in many respects, particularly as regards awarding costs, sufficiently attest the fact that they were influenced in their decisions, have been influenced, by nothing but their own individual will and caprice. I fear very much that the practical result of the Sub-Commissions hitherto has been to fill the minds of the tenants with an amount of excitement and vague expectation, which must be most prejudicial to the hope of future harmony and peace in the country ; and, moreover, must be most injurious to all parties concerned, from the prospect of interminable litigation which it is sure to produce and encourage.

I feel now that I have intruded long enough on your indulgence, and there must be gentlemen around me far more competent than I am to dicuss this question, and whose opinions we must all be anxious to hear. I shall, therefore, now proceed, in conclusion, to read the words of the resolution which I have to propose for your adoption :—

" That this meeting, while expressing its unalterable attachment to the Crown and Constitution of the realm, and the readiness of the landowners of Ireland, as loyal subjects, to submit to the provisions of the Land Law (Ireland) Act, sees with alarm that that measure is being at present administered in a manner at variance with the pledge that it would not diminish the value or disturb the foundations of property, and contrary to the assurances on the faith of which Parliament was advised not to provide compensation."

on rising to second the resolution, was received with prolonged cheers. He said—

My Lord Duke, my Lords and Gentlemen—In seconding this resolution, I shall not say one word upon the policy of the Land Act of last session, however much I may deplore that policy. The Act has passed both Houses of Parliament, and has received the sanction of the Sovereign, and, as law-abiding subjects, we are bound to submit to its authority. It is only with the manner in which that measure is being administered that we have to deal to-day ; and, in supporting this resolution, I desire more particularly to show that the measure adopted has already produced, and, if persevered in, must continue to produce consequences absolutely at variance with the pledges which were given by her Majesty's Ministers when they introduced their Bill, and contrary to the assurances upon the faith of which Parliament was induced to pass it into law. I pass by the action of those Commissioners who were named in the Bill, although I think that all fair-minded men must deeply regret the language used by the Chief-Commissioner when opening his court. That language appeared to me most dangerous, and to foreshadow much of the mischief which has followed. Their authority has, however, for the present been transferred to a number of Sub-Commissioners for the purpose of determining judicial rents ; and it is with the question of these judicial rents that we are at this moment immediately and urgently concerned.

We have watched for weeks with ever-increasing surprise and alarm the proceedings of these Assistant Commissioners, until the conviction has been irresistibly forced upon us that these gentlemen have undertaken—not seriously—to revalue particular farms, but set up new standards for the fixing of rentals through Ireland, and to encourage the people to believe that by availing themselves of their courts they would secure without fail substantial reductions of those rents which under their existing contracts they were bound to pay. And what up to the present have been the practical results? I am informed that a reduction of about twenty-five per cent. has been made over the four provinces, and in Connaught, which I know best, the result of the cases hitherto decided is a reduction of twenty-nine per cent., leaving the rental actually under Griffith's valuation; and I may mention that the whole increase of rent amounts, for the province of Ulster, to £12 12s.; for Leinster, 10s.; Munster, nothing; Connaught, nothing. In these cases are included rents which have not been raised for long periods.

It is obvious that if these decisions be not speedily reversed on appeal they will be steadily followed in future; and once a new standard has been thus established by law, and a new and artificial level for rents has been fixed by these Sub-Commissions, it will be imperative for other landlords to conform, in order to save the useless costs of a lawsuit with each of their tenants, and to reduce their rents, not because they doubt the justice of their cause, but because they cannot afford the expense of disputing what will be really a foregone conclusion. And thus the practical outcome must, so far as I can judge, be a general reduction of rents throughout Ireland of an average of at least twenty-five per cent. Startling and serious as such a loss of income must be, even in the cases of the wealthy, and of those who may derive part of their means from other sources—with that numerous body of Irish proprietors whose incomes are solely drawn from the land, and who are burthened with heavy family charges, insurances, and other incumbrances— it will mean absolute beggary and ruin. I need hardly add that under such circumstances Irish estates are absolutely unsaleable.

Now, gentlemen, I pray your attention and the honest judgment of all fair-minded men while I show you that these results of the administration of this measure are directly contrary to the solemn pledges—the confident and reiterated assurances—which were given by Her Majesty's Government when the Bill was before Parliament, and on the faith of which Parliament passed this Act, without providing compensation to those who might suffer from it. In Her Majesty's most gracious speech this measure was spoken of as one which "should not diminish the value or disturb the foundations of property." Again, Mr. Gladstone, in his speech introducing the Land Bill, said that he could not have justified such a measure, " on the ground, whether expressed or implied, of general misconduct on the part of the Irish landlords." He said that " they had stood their trial, and, as a rule, they had been acquitted," and he added, " It may seem hard, where there are so many landlords with whom we have not a shred of title to interfere, were it possible to sever their case from other cases around them, that they must be liable to interference on account of the acts or omissions of the few"; and similar confident statements were made again and again during the progress of the measure. And they were justified in holding such language, and Parliament was justified in accepting it, for the Bessborough Commission and the Richmond Commission had both found that credit was due to the Irish landlords as a class for not exacting all that they were entitled to exact from their tenantry. Is it not absurd to measure against the value of such testimony the hasty surveys, the haphazard decisions of the Assistant Commissioners who are now re-arranging off-hand the rental of Ireland ?

There is one other topic alluded to in this resolution; it is that of compensation. I know how strongly that subject must stir the minds of those assembled here to-day, and there is no one of you who feels more strongly than I do the irresistible justice of that demand in case the proceedings of the Assistant-Commissioners should be sanctioned, and the consequences which I have spoken of should follow; but I join earnestly in the advice of our noble chairman that the time has not yet come for pressing that claim, and I feel confident that we shall best consult our own interests and dignity by simply adhering for the present to the resolutions which are upon the paper. We say it is one thing to carry a Bill through Parliament to prevent individual cases of oppression, and another thing to use it in order to work a political and social revolution. The Legislature might, no doubt, have seen fit frankly to enact that for the pacification of Ireland one-fourth of the income of the landowners should be transferred to their tenants; but if so no one would have questioned the right of the former to immediate and complete compensation. It might have been the will of Parliament to fix the rental of Ireland at the Government valuation, or at ten per cent. or any other value it pleased above or below that standard; but if such sweeping changes by force of law had reduced the incomes of the landowners, means must necessarily be found to make good that deficiency.

Let me quote on this subject a few strong words spoken by Mr. Gladstone in the House of Commons on the 22nd of July, when he opposed a motion made by Sir Walter Barttelot on this subject:—"I do not hesitate to say that if it can be shown on clear and definite experience at the present time that there is a probability, or, if after experience should prove that, in fact, ruin and heavy loss is likely to be, or has been, brought upon any class in Ireland by the direct effect of this legislation—that is a question which we ought to look very directly in the face." And again—"As I stated, my opinion was that the operation of the Bill would in many cases have the effect of raising the rents, and thereby creating discontent. I quite agree that if Parliament were to pass a law providing that rents in Ireland should be universally reduced to Griffith's valuation, that would be a fair case for compensation."

My Lords and Gentlemen, I have shown that the proceedings of the Assistant-Commissioners up to the present have produced results differing scarcely by a degree from those described in these words of the Prime Minister; and, if their action should be sanctioned, we shall appeal with confidence to the honour and justice of Parliament and Englishmen to redress the grave injury which would otherwise be done to law-abiding subjects of the Queen by this Act.

LORD JAMES BUTLER,

who rose in the body of the hall to address the meeting, was received with loud applause. He then proceeded to the platform in compliance with calls from various parts of the hall. He said—

My Lord Duke, my Lords, Ladies and Gentlemen—Anybody who has listened attentively to the words that have fallen from his Grace, and those who have already spoken, cannot but agree that we have met here in a state of affairs in this country unparalleled entirely, I believe, in any country which has the slightest pretence to a representative assembly. With the resolution, to which I shall move an amendment, I, and I suppose those here present, will agree as to the spirit, but not as to the wording. It is difficult, as was mentioned just now, to realize what the suffering must be in the case of those who, with large estates, are suddenly deprived of from one quarter up to I believe as high as seventy-five per cent. of the income from those estates. Are these not the people who are really suffering at this moment? Let anybody look around and see the result of this Land Act, and the way in which it is being carried on in this country; let anyone look to the feeling it has given rise to in England— to the societies that have sprung up to relieve distress, and put a fire on the fireless hearths, and to enable parents in some instances to maintain themselves out of the workhouse. When we ponder over these things we say, although we may agree with some of the wording of this resolution, is it sufficient to meet the whole case? I say it is not. I express no opinion in sugared words; these are not times to use them. The resolution expresses the readiness of the landowners of Ireland to submit. Well, I think they submit with the same amount of readiness that a soldier exhibits when he strips at the halberts to receive three hundred lashes. It may be tolerated by some, but that is another thing.

I have read letters from those connected with the Government in other places—holding positions under the Government— who look smilingly, who, being absentee landlords themselves, on the sufferings of many in this country, feeling assured that, although the rent may not be paid, the official quarter-day may not fail them possibly yet. I do not consider that the words of the resolution are suitable to the particular occasion, and I wish, therefore, to make a slight variation in the language. It is all nonsense not to express an opinion on the Act itself, while we denounce in every sort of way the manner in which that Act is being carried out. I conceive that there ought to be a further addition to this resolution, pledging this assembly, as far as it can do, to work together in order, if possible, to obtain a reform or modification of the Act itself. It must be in the minds of many that this is perfectly constitutional; and, strange to say, this morning I find in a letter from one certainly not too favourable, I think, to the landlords of Ireland—Mr. Chamberlain—that he speaks of the Government looking with approval on the means being used to obtain the reform of an unjust law. If that does not warrant us in taking as strong action as we can on this subject, I do not know what words would be sufficient.

What is the whole of this Act based on ? If anyone made inquiry in regard to the tenure of land in Ireland, it would be found that the landlords were acquitted over and over again by him who brought in the Act; and yet their property is being swept away from them by men who are so highly unfitted for the duties they have been appointed to discharge, that their appointments are an insult to common sense. It is an insult to common sense to conceive the selection of such men for such posts. The amendment that I propose to the resolution will come in after the word " and " in the second line, and is as follows :—

" The bounden duty of every loyal subject to obey the law." I move that these words should take the place of the following words in the resolution, viz.:—"The readiness of the landowners of Ireland as loyal subjects to submit to the provisions of the Land Law (Ireland) Act." Then, at the close of the resolution, after that unhappy word " compensation," I move that we add the words—" That this great meeting pledges itself by every constitutional means to obtain a modification and reform of an unjust law." It is lawful to borrow from the enemy, and I quote these words from Mr. Chamberlain's letter—" And, further, to uphold the rights of all kinds of property, and to maintain freedom of contract and liberty of action between man and man in this realm." I beg to move that as an amendment.

The Right Hon. EDWARD GIBSON, M.P.—His Grace has requested me to act as his assessor at this meeting, and to advise him as to the form of amendments and their legality; and I am of opinion that the first part of the resolution moved by Lord James Butler, which purposes to substitute a new clause in the first part of the sentence of the resolution, is in order, and may be moved. I am of opinion that the words he proposes to be added after the word "compensation," at the end of the resolution, are clearly out of order, and cannot be moved. This is a meeting summoned to consider the administration of the existing law, not to propose or accept amendments in favour of new laws; and therefore the second part of Lord James Butler's amendment cannot be moved. The formal way in which his Grace will present the question to the meeting is this. He will ask you whether you are in favour of omitting the words in the resolution—"The readiness of the landlords of Ireland as loyal subjects to submit to the provisions of the Land Act," &c., and substituting instead the words proposed by Lord James Butler, or whether the words proposed to be left out should stand part of the resolution.

MR. ROBERT STAPLES (Durrow)

seconded the amendment, which was put to the meeting and negatived.

The resolution, as it originally stood, was next put, and adopted.

THE MARQUIS OF WATERFORD moved—

" That the position, antecedents, experience, and status of the Assistant-Commissioners should be such as to insure the impartial and judicial exercise of their functions, and to command the confidence of suitors and of the public; and this meeting observes that in many of the appointments by which these offices have been filled the above considerations appear to have been overlooked."

He said—I have much pleasure in moving this resolution, because I think it is high time the public were made aware how one of the most important promises made at the time of the passing of the Land Act has been carried out, and that the result of the nomination of the Sub-Commissioners, as shown by their decisions, is entirely at variance with the promises made by the Government when they advocated the adoption of that measure. This, I consider, a most serious matter, because if the decisions of the Sub-Commissioners are not reversed upon appeal—and I hear now that there is even some question in reference to appeals except upon points of law—the result will be very serious indeed. I can hardly believe that that will be the case. Suppose, however, that Griffith's valuation should become the standard of the rents in Ireland, I believe that a large number of Irish landed proprietors will be absolutely, totally, and entirely ruined, and they and their families will be obliged either to take refuge in the workhouse or beg their bread from door to door.

We have been told by his Grace, and by other speakers, that this is not a political meeting, and I think it would be a great pity if the question of politics should be raised. We are not met here to demand that law and order should be re-established in this distracted country, much as we may wish that that might be the case. We are not met here to find fault with the Government for having passed the Land Act or any other measure. We have met here calmly and dispassionately to consider the administration of a statute, which having passed into law, we as law-abiding citizens—and we are proud of being law-abiding citizens—should accept and obey, as we have accepted and obeyed other Acts of Parliament which have become law in the land.

Well, gentlemen, there was no statement so often reiterated by Government as that the court to fix fair rents should be an able and impartial tribunal, and it will be for the public to judge, after they have heard the statements so ably made to-day, whether that promise has been carried out, or whether in the nomination of the Sub-Commissioners it has not been thrown to the winds. Can anybody say from the previous history of many of the Sub-Commissioners that they are likely to form courts of impartial tribunal? And do not their decisions bear out exactly what was expected from their previous history. These Sub-Commissioners, mark you, were appointed by the Government and not by Parliament; and I have seen lately in the public prints—I do not know how true it may be—that they have received orders from the Government as to how they are to act. Therefore, the Government is entirely responsible for their decisions. Does their appointment agree with Mr. Gladstone's statement when introducing the Bill, and when he said—"The court must not be a one-sided court. We cannot

make those who sit on the seat of justice forsake justice, even
with objects so high as the object of Land Reform in Ireland."
Lord Carlingford and other members of the Government stated
exactly the same thing, and it is unnecessary for me to weary
you with quotations. Every member of the Government in
every speech made repeated that assurance, and I am satisfied
that Parliament never would have passed the Land Act except
for those promises. Over and over again the Government
stated that this court, which was to exercise higher powers
than any court since the days of the Star Chamber, were to be
the most able and impartial men that could be found. I would
ask you are tenant-farmers likely to be impartial at any time in
judging land cases, and especially in a time like the present?
Are gentlemen who have given vent to the strongest opinions
against the landlords likely to be impartial? I believe many
of the appointments have been made mainly because of such
opinions and pronouncements. We find several members—or
I believe, at all events one or two—of Mr. Porter's committee
among the Sub-Commissioners ; and I suppose those gentlemen
endorse the statements which appeared in the Solicitor-General's
address. I would like to know are the Government likely to
get the most able men in Ireland for the salary they are giving,
and when many of the appointments are only made for a-year?
This question of appointment for a year is a most important
point, because ever since the days of the Revolution the Judges
of the British Empire—of the British Isles at any rate—have
been appointed during their good behaviour, that is for life
practically. But these Judges, who are to have the most extraordinary powers over an enormous amount of property, are
appointed merely for a year ; therefore, at the end of the year, if
they do not carry out the directions given them by the Government which we hear of, what will be said to them ? The Government—their masters—will say, " Go about your business—we
withdraw the salary which we have given you." Those gentlemen, no doubt, have given up their professions to take these
salaries—small as I consider they are for the work to be performed, and they will be ready, rather than lose them, if such an
alternative be set before them, to follow the orders of the
Government. I do not call that an impartial tribunal.

Lord Selborne and Lord Carlingford, in urging that there would be no difficulty whatsoever in fixing a fair rent, stated that the Court should be composed of most able and experienced men, "assisted"—mark this—"by competent valuators and surveyors." I would like to know are the Sub-Commissioners experienced men in the matter of valuing land? I have received a letter from a gentleman since I entered this hall, who says that the only knowledge one of the Sub-Commissioners had of the land in his district was, that he had a very small garden. This business of valuing land, we all know, will take an able man many years to learn. But if we want a proof of how inexperienced the Sub-Commissioners are, we could find it in the manner in which they are pursuing their work. Where are the valuers and experts that we were promised by the Government? They have never appeared at all, and I think it is not difficult to account for their absence, because if the Government called in first-class men—honest men of that profession, the Sub-Commissioners would not be able to carry out their orders. Then the authorities would be told the fair letting value of the land, a fact which they now seem to wish to ignore.

I consider it, as the noble Duke has said in his able speech, positively a monstrous thing, that three gentlemen unacquainted with a district, and in the dead of winter, after having heard a certain amount of evidence on the tenant's side—not very difficult to obtain—and a few witnesses on the landlord's side—almost impossible in the state of the country to obtain—should proceed to give a decision on the rent of a farm on walking through a few fields, or spending (as the noble chairman mentioned) a couple of hours in looking at it, when a clever valuer with a scale of prices before him would take several days to do the work. Is it not clear to every man in this country what the reasons are upon which those Sub-Commissioners are basing their decisions, and that those decisions can have nothing to do with the cursory glances at a farm? and they could have nothing certainly to do with the evidence given, because they were generally entirely against the evidence. They tell you that they are proceeding upon a certain principle, however, and it is not difficult to know what that principle is. They are reducing the rents of Ireland something below Griffith's valuation, merely varying them a little to prove to the British public—I don't think they care a bit about the Irish public—that they are not proceeding upon those lines. I don't think it is necessary for me to define what Griffith's valuation is. That is well known. But Mr. Gladstone himself quoted from the Bessborough Commission that "Griffith's valuation was very much below the fair letting value of the land, and that it was no guide whatsoever as to rents." Why did the Prime Minister go out of his way to make such a quotation if he did not believe it was the case? and I don't think he, at any rate, could have given the orders to the Sub-Commissioners, whatever the Irish Executive may have done. Did the Government lead Parliament to believe that the rents of Ireland would be very much reduced? Nothing of the kind.

We were led to believe that this Act was necessary, not for the purpose of reducing the rents of the bulk of the landlords of Ireland, but for the purpose of reducing the rents of those who had rack-rented their tenants. Lord Carlingford spoke most strongly upon this point, although now, indeed, at Frome not long ago he seems to have said that Griffith's valuation is a fair rent for a great deal of the land of Ireland, only, apparently, excepting very few of the rich grazing lands. He must have formed a very different opinion on the 1st of August, when he must have been as well aware as he is now that the rents of Ireland are very much above Griffith's valuation, and that even the rents on what have been called by him and other members of the Government liberally managed estates are very much above Griffith's valuation. Knowing so much as he did about the state of Ireland, he says, on the 1st of August:—"I maintain that the provisions of this Bill will cost the landlords no money loss whatever. I believe that it will inflict on them no loss of income, except in those cases in which a certain number of landlords may have imposed on their tenants excessive and inequitable rents." I cannot understand how a responsible Minister could have made two such distinct and different statements as the one which he made on the 1st of August in the House of Lords, and the one which he made at Frome a fortnight ago. Would Lord Carlingford, or would anybody, dare to say that almost every case that has come before the Courts up to the present time has been upon the property of a rack-renter, and that the whole of Ireland is let at rack-rents, because that is absolutely what these decisions amount to? The fact of the matter is, as the noble duke pointed out, the whole of the proceedings of these impartial tribunals amount to a farce, which one would laugh at were it not for the other side, which renders them a tragedy so frightful for the hopes, happiness, property, prosperity, and the very lives of many I see before me in this room, and many friends of ours who are in the country, that it is perfectly frightful to contemplate.

We know very well that a great number of Irish estates are charged up to three-fourths of their rent-roll—or, at least, two-thirds of their rent-roll; and if the one-third that the landed proprietors lived upon is taken away, it is not difficult to guess the result. Can the Government, can Parliament, can the British people be aware of how this Act is being administered, so totally different from what the one side and the other were led to expect? Is this the boasted English justice which has been our pride for generations, and which has also been one of the causes of our past prosperity—that the property of one class, purchased under Government guarantee so called, is to be taken away for the benefit of another? Is this the way that the landlords' properties are to be restored and increased, according to the Lord Chancellor? Is this the great boon to all parties that this Act was to be, according to Lord Carlingford; and will the landlords of Ireland generally find themselves exactly in the same position as the landlords of Ulster before the Act was passed, according to the same authority? Cannot damage be proved now, if these decisions be not reversed upon appeal, and loss of income, for which, if it were proved, Mr. Gladstone said compensation might be demanded from the public funds? Other members of the Government said what was tantamount to the same thing—that as there was no loss there need be no compensation—therefore admitting that if there were a loss there should be compensation. What we demand is justice; impartial justice is all that we require.

Let our cases be heard at once, before it is too late, upon appeal. If it be found by the Commissioners—the men appointed by Parliament to fix the rents of Ireland, although up to the present time they have not fixed one single rent—and if it be found necessary to reduce our incomes, contrary to the promises made to Parliament, and contrary to all fairness and justice— then at least let them give us compensation for what they are taking from us. And if they will not listen to our appeal, and will not check the Sub-Commissioners in the ruin which tracks their course, no one can ever believe in their promises again, and the name and fame of English justice will soon fade into the distant past, blasted and destroyed by the provisions of an Act passed by him who has been the most eloquent advocate of justice in the world.

MR. RICHARD J. MAHONY.

My Lord Duke, my Lords, and Gentlemen, there is but one word to which I will take exception in the able speech of the noble proposer of this resolution, which has been justly received by this meeting, and that word is this, that he "accepts" this Act. So far as a private individual could go, I resisted this Bill from the first. Now that it has passed, I do not "accept" it; I do not approve of it; I do not acquiesce in it; but in that word, most admirably chosen in this resolution, I "submit" to it. I was one of those who ventured to hope that while wrong—it has been said grievous wrong existed in Ireland—while wrong would be redressed, yet that the dangerous principles inherent in this Act would be minimized by those intrusted with the administration of it. I regret to stand here this day and to renounce that belief. I believe, and I say it with sorrow and disappointment, that there is no status left in Ireland for a working landowner. There are men—men in this assembly—who for many years past —for the greater part of their lives—have cast what they had of enterprise and capital into the cause of their country. In other lands such a course would have brought them profit and honour. If it does not here it is not because of agitation. Agitation is a great and terrible evil, but it may be faced, it may be resisted, it may be overcome, if you have law as well as justice on your side. But if confidence fails in the laws of the land, on what basis will you restore society ?

My Lord, a short time ago some of us may have seen in the newspapers an account of an experiment in architectural engineering attempted in America. There was a great building, with a façade of some hundreds of feet, and the same extent in depth—a building that had grown up for years of massive work. Storey after storey had been added. Within this building there was a whole community of interests — warehouses, shops, hotels; it towered up to the skies. The idea was by some wonderful triumph of engineering to raise up this building from below, and to move it out of its place into another site prepared for it. It was a great undertaking, and the highest, the best opinions in engineering in the land were chosen, and rightly chosen, to superintend such a work. Engineers were told off to watch the whole face of this great building, so that the smallest settlement might be seen at once and provided against; and at last, when everything was prepared, the great experiment was undertaken; the wedges were driven underneath, and it was raised up from its foundations; and then began the great work of moving it, slowly, exactly according to the arrangements laid out from the beginning—inch by inch, a few inches a day, and at last it was moved into its selected berth. Something like that was the attempt made last Session to move an interest in this country that had grown for centuries —an interest that had been, generation after generation, added to by the industry of each successive generation—an interest that was founded deep in the very foundations of the Constitution. And what was the time that was chosen for this experiment in statesmanship? It was a time when a hurricane was blowing over the land. Is that a time to put such an interest upon rollers, when it may be carried away out of the direction which its promoters intended from the beginning, so as to crush every fabric around it in one undistinguishable ruin? Yet, such was the experiment that was attempted, and what had been the result?

I am sure we can all remember with what breathless expectation Parliament and the whole country waited day after day to hear from the Prime Minister the names of those eminent men who were to be instructed with the great task of engineering this great movement, and when at last their names were announced there was a sigh of relief; and not only when their names were heard—that was not the only guarantee that Mr. Gladstone gave that this great undertaking should be conducted with proper discretion, but also he himself gave us an assurance that they would touch with reverence this great fabric of the Constitution, regarding which they were intrusted with the task of undertaking such an experiment. Then, my Lord, who were those chosen to carry out this design?—who were those intrusted with this tremendous task? They had to lay out the whole plan of operations, they had to draw the plans, to form the very machinery, and what was the time at which this was done? There was a whole multitude waiting, watching impatiently for the experiment. Time pressed. The will of the majority in these days is as imperious and absolute as was ever the will of old Nebuchadnezzar or Nero. There was an anxious multitude pressing up to the very barriers, watching the chimney tops and the turrets for the time when they would see them vibrate against the sky line. Where were the engineers chosen to carry out the experiment carefully, trustfully? A number of volunteers came forth from the multitude—we know their antecedents; they came forth with the very feelings, impressions, and desires of those standing around waiting to see the experiment, and reckless as to what would be the result. They were chosen, and on what principle? In these days there is scarcely an employment of the very smallest consequence which is not subject to a competitive contest. Was there any examination, any competitive test whatsoever of these gentlemen? We read of none. They went forth to their work—I do not know with what qualifications. I do not think they have proved their qualification: but they went forth certainly with what is said to be the better part of discretion—they went forth with sufficient valour. They have proved that. Well, what was the first task with which they were intrusted? They were intrusted with the task of fixing fair rents. What are fair rents? How are fair rents to be measured? Have you anything to measure them by except the law of supply and demand? These gentlemen, I think, are scarcely to be blamed, for they were put to decide what mathematicians would call an unknown quantity. If you were to apply the same rule to England, if you were to send a number of Commissionners to England to carry out the same law there, do we not know that the result would be even more startling than in Ireland, for Mr. Caird, a high authority on agricultural matters, tells us that the rents in Ireland are twenty-five per cent. below the rents of all Europe. If this be the case, I suppose if they were sent to apply this test in England you would have rents reduced some fifty per cent. But, my lord, how is this carried out? We are not to get the *coup de grace* at once; there is no mercy in this execution Year by year the agony is to be prolonged. They are to circle round in one vicious circle. I don't know whether this generation will see the end of it. It is something like the Chinese punishment for murder, and we are to be pulled to pieces, bit by bit, and that by unscientific operators.

My Lord, we have been told, and I am sure correctly, that the rents of Ireland will be reduced twenty-five per cent.—that is, of those as yet untried. That is foreshadowed; so that all the rest of Ireland which has not yet been put into the dock is already pronounced guilty. But where is the real criminal? The real criminal walks at large in England. It is only in Ireland that he is refused a place. The real criminal is political economy. If he be found within the precints of the courts he is conducted to the doors, and he is banished to Saturn. I do not believe that at present, with all its greatness, England is diplomatically represented in that distant planet, and I do not think there is sufficient influence with the authorities there to detain the criminal. My Lord, he will return, and he will return with a vengeance, and his watchword will be, "Nemo me impune lacessit." You cannot make a law which will prevent his return; and I warn you that you will see rack-rents in Ireland higher than ever they have been yet. Alongside of fair rents you will see rack-rents growing up. I will tell you why. The other day a prominent Land Leaguer in the South of Ireland said to a friend of mine, "This Land Act will be the ruin of the farmers, for it will procure them greater credit than they ever had before." And so it will. One class is put out of the way, but for all the rest there remains this power of rack-renting. The ex-owner becomes an annuitant; he has no further interest in that which once belonged to him; but then come in the merchant, the trader, the usurer, and the gombeen man. These will command the situation; these are the future rulers of the land. You will re-establish the institution that has been admitted on all hands to be the very ruin of our country, for you will bring back the middleman.

Well, my lord, we are gathered here this day, as has been said so well by Lord Waterford, only to ask for justice—simple justice—the justice of fair trial, which is not refused to the worst of criminals. If justice is refused to us, our alternative is not sedition. The historical motto of those who are gathered here this day has been " Faithful though not favoured." I will tell you the alternative which we have, and it is one consistent with loyalty. In the dark days of our country—we look back upon them now as dark days—I think they were lighter than the present. In one respect they were darker then, for there was not the union, which I am glad to see here to-day, amongst those who must, if the country is ever to prosper, be the natural leaders of law. In those dark days the light of the dawn of liberty was still breaking on the horizon, and in those days an illustrious band of exiles came to Ireland. She opened her arms to receive them; they came from a land from which they had been driven by oppression and ignorant legislation; they brought with them industry, and enterprise, and capital, and with this they repaid the land that took them to her arms and to her heart. I am sure there are before me this day representatives of those exiles—names that are associated with a full share of everything that is great, that is noble, and that is worthy in our land; and if we look back across generations to the ancestral traditions of another land, we will see that the impress of Irish nativity has stamped them with the characteristics of our common country. Is it to be said that their descendants will have to record the story of another emigration—an emigration from the land of their ancestors' adoption, and because of the same oppressive laws? Is it to be said that capital and enterprise will leave this land in search of freer soil? I don't know what foreign shore awaits those exiles of Erin, but this I may say, it will not be a country where the laws of the land confiscate private investment—where they violate solemn contract, and where, by proscribing private, and individual, and absolute ownership of property—whether inherited or acquired—they root up the very foundations on which the wealth of nations is built.

The resolution was then put and carried unanimously.

MR. ARTHUR M‘M. KAVANAGH,

who was warmly received, proposed the next resolution. He said—

Upon me devolves the task of moving the fourth resolution; and although I would have been glad that this duty had fallen upon some other person more competent to do justice to it, I am not sorry to have the opportunity afforded to me of saying a few words about it. Occupying the position which I lately held, as a member of the Bessborough Commission, and recommending, as I did, the system of arbitration for the settlement of disputes as to rent, I feel that, in the opinion of some, I may be charged with pursuing an inconsistent course in recommending the adoption of a system at one time, and at another asking you to pass a resolution condemning its effect. But in the resolution which I have now the honour to propose I do not ask you to condemn the principle that is now embodied in an Act of Parliament, and as loyal subjects we are, in my opinion, bound to abide by it. More than that, the principle is one which I endorse myself, and the necessity for its adoption I am still prepared to maintain. It is not the principle, then, that I ask you to condemn by this resolution, but the manner in which it is administered; and I believe I shall have no difficulty in proving that it is such as neither the framers of the Bill, nor the Parliament that passed it into an Act, ever contemplated.

I will briefly state the grounds upon which I make this assertion. First, we have in the Queen's Speech, when referring to the Bill to be introduced dealing with the Irish land question, the pledge that it would not diminish the value or disturb the foundations of property. We have, second, Mr. Gladstone's words, spoken on the 7th of April—" Well, sir, neither, I am bound to say, should we think it just to propose legislation on the ground, whether expressed or implied, of general misconduct on the part of the landlords of Ireland. On the contrary, as a rule, they have stood their trial, and, as a rule, they have been acquitted. The report of the Bessborough Commission, which certainly is not deficient in its popular sympathies, declares that the greatest credit is due to the Irish landlords for not exacting all that by law they were entitled to exact." We have further his words, spoken on July 22nd, referring to some previous debate—"As I then stated, my opinion was that the operation of the Bill would, in many cases, have the effect of raising the rents, and thereby causing discontent." I quote Mr. Gladstone, not only on account of his great ability, or of the immense weight attaching to any utterance of his as Prime Minister, but more especially from the fact that he was the sole author of the Bill—this one Bill of a protracted session. Mr. Gladstone, and Mr. Gladstone alone, was in charge of the measure, and conducted it through its difficult course, from its introduction to its third reading; therefore his opinions and speeches are of peculiar significance. I could quote to you words from Lord Selborne's speeches when the measure reached the House of Lords. I could quote to you paragraphs from the main report of the Bessborough Commissioners to the effect that "the large estates," which you will remember comprise the majority of agricultural holdings in the country, "were well and considerately managed." That means that there was no unjust exaction of rent. But I do not want to occupy your time by multiplying quotations. I have given you enough to show that those who originated the Bill, and suggested the necessity for its introduction, were of opinion that the majority of rents were not unreasonable. I have given you Mr. Gladstone's words, clearly showing that, in his opinion, the effect of the Bill would certainly not be the wholesale and universal reduction of rents. On that assumption, the question of compensation was not then dealt with. But leaving the subject of the rents for a moment, there is another and a most material point in my argument which I must bring before you, and that is as to the impartial nature of the tribunal who have to decide this vital question of fair rent. I can again bring Mr. Gladstone's words to my assistance. On

July 22nd, when referring to the subject of compensation he spoke thus :—" If it be that compensation is to be demanded under that clause, because a judicial rent and a statutory term are about to be determined, all I can say is, that a judicial rent can only be fixed and a statutory term can only be established according to the judgment of a dispassionate and impartial judicial body, who will have to decide between man and man according to the facts proved before them." Now, these are the two facts upon which I base my argument, viz.—that the Bill was passed on the assurance and the understanding that there would be no universal reduction of rent, and that the tribunal would be a dispassionate and impartial one.   But what are the facts that we are met here to-day to consider? Have we got a dispassionate and impartial tribunal? In the answer to that question the entire issue is bound up.   In the Head Commissioners I would be sorry to think that we had not ; but of these Sub-Commissions—those species of flying columns, who deal arbitrarily with our means of living—I am disposed to think differently.   Personally I have not a word to say about any one of them.   What their qualifications are, or why they were selected, I know nothing, save what rumour gives ; but although ignorant on those points, I am not, I believe, entirely in the dark as to the instructions they have received to guide their actions. I believe—and I am glad of being able now to make this statement publicly, in order that her Majesty's Government may have the opportunity of contradicting it if it is not correct—I believe there have been secret instructions of a very grave nature, their acceptance of and their compliance with which is a condition of their appointment.   As to the nature of those instructions I am, of course, as much in the dark as any of the general public, but even on this point we are not without some gleam of light.

I will read an extract from the letter of the correspondent of the *Standard*, obviously and notoriously written in support of these Sub-Commissioners, and in defence of their administration of this Act.   It was written on December 26th, 1881, and gave, as the "Principles of determining fair rent" — First, to carry out Healy's clause as liberally as possible.   Second, when neither landlord nor tenant had im-

proved the holding, but the landlord had, without apparent
cause, raised the rent, to restore it to its original figure. Third,
where no improvement or raising of rent, or no other distinct
index of value, to fall back on Griffith's valuation. Now, these
instructions, when compared with the decisions of the Sub-Commissioners, would certainly seem to me to be inspired, and I
think I am right in assuming that they are more than a mere
haphazard guess. But there is a further light thrown on them,
and from a source which makes it more than ordinarily ominous ; and I must—although I deprecate anything having the
appearance of party politics being imported into our discussion
—I must refer to the late Derry election and to some speeches
made by Mr. Porter, the present Solicitor-General, during his
canvass on that occasion. At a meeting at Magherafelt on
November 17th, Mr. Porter stated " that the Land Act was
passed because the fact was forced on the attention of the
Legislature of Great Britain that the vast bulk of the land
in this country was excessively over-rented." This he asserts
as a fact more than once. All I can say is, that if it is a fact,
it is one which neither of the Royal Commissions that sat to
inquire into the question discovered. At Limavady on November 21st Mr. Porter uses these words, and they are very ominous
words :—" Some of the Assistant-Commissioners who had the
power of fixing a fair rent had been appointed for seven
years, but a great many had only been appointed for one year."
At Cookstown on November 26th he said " he had seen in some
cases where the Sub-Commissioners had reduced the rents, it appeared to him that they had not reduced them sufficiently."
    Now I must ask, What do these words prove ? Are they not
a clear threat to those Sub-Commissioners who have been appointed for only one year, that if they did not act in sympathy
with the Government and reduce rents they would not be re-
appointed ? Now, take the decisions of these Sub-Commissioners as far as they have gone. I have a return here showing the
number of cases in which judicial rents have been fixed by the
Assistant-Commissioners up to the 31st December. So far as
returns have been received up to that date, the total number
of cases in which judicial rents have been fixed is 645. The
acreage dealt with was 19,717 acres ; the old rents amounted to

£17,391 15s. 11d. ; the new rents amount to £13,085 2s. 10d., and the gross amount of the reductions, £4322 15s. 3d., or 24.8 per cent. In Ulster there were 305 cases heard; the old rent was £6475 15s. 9d. ; the new rent amounts to £4914 1s. 7d. ; and the gross amount of the reductions is £1577 6s. 4d. In Ulster we have three bright spots called increases, to which I shall refer hereafter. In Leinster there were 66 cases heard. The old rent in these cases amounted to £2310 15s. 11d. ; the new rent has been fixed at £1736 17s. 11d., showing a gross reduction of £574 8s. In Munster there were 159 cases heard, and the old rent amounted to £7178 11s. 3d. The new rent has been fixed at £5418 7s. 9d., the gross amount of the reductions being £1760 3s. 6d. In Connaught 115 cases were heard, and the old rents were reduced from £1426 13s. to £1015 15s. 7d., showing a total reduction of £410 17s. 5d.

Now, I will shortly refer to the cases that have not been decreased, but rather increased. These amount to five in number, and the total amount of the increase is £16 2s. 2d. Of these five cases, four were in Ulster and one in Leinster. The following facts referring to each are worth noting. The first case is Sir Oriel Foster's half-crown. Sir Oriel Foster was the landlord, and the tenant was named Mary M'Ardle. The gross acreage of the farm was 12A. 0R. 39P. The old rent was £3 15s. ; poor law valuation, £5 ; and the new rent, as fixed by the Assistant-Commissioners at Castleblayney, is £3 17s. 6d. Mr. M'Bride, the landlord's valuator, swore that the fair rent should be £4 9s. 8d., excluding all the tenant's improvements. The tenant was evicted for four years' rent, and at the time of the decision of the Assistant-Commissioners the amount due represented four and a-half years' rent. The landlord had to abide his own costs. Forty years of the additional rent, if paid, would not recoup the landlord for his costs of being brought into court, though his rent was raised instead of diminished ! The second increase was the result of a mistake of law, under which Sub-Commission No. 2 laboured. The case was decided at Lisburn. The tenant was Alexander Creighton, and the landlord was Horatio Nelson, of Downpatrick. The acreage of the holding was 25A. 0R. 25P. statute. The old rent was £27 4s. ; the poor-law valuation £26 ; and the new rent, as fixed by the Sub-Commissioners, is £29 2s. 6d. The chairman of the Sub-Commission stated that they had made this increase instead of the slight increase which the landlord said he was willing to accept, " because henceforth in all cases where judicial rents were fixed the landlord would have to pay half the county cess; and as the holding was worth much more, and to keep the landlord safe with respect to the county cess, they had increased the rent by £1 18s. 6d." This was a mistake of law, and the tenant has appealed. The third increase was made under a similar mistake of law, by the same Sub-Commission, at Newry. The tenant in that case was R. N. Mullen, and the landlord the Earl of Kilruddery. The acreage was 32A. 1R. 23P.; the old rent, £38 14s 4d.; poor-law valuation £38; and the new rent has been settled at £41 14s. The Sub-Commissioners believed at the time of the decision that the increase would only repay the landlord with respect to the county cess. The reductions during the first six weeks of this Sub-Commission (No. 2) were under 25 per cent. The Commissioners stated several times in court, and in about nineteen cases actually ordered, that the landlord should pay half the county cess during the statutory term. This meant an additional loss of five per cent. to the landlord. During the last two or three weeks it has become clear that the landlord may not have to pay half the county cess, and the reductions of this Commission have been accordingly increased, and have averaged 28 per cent. since. The fourth increase was at Bailieborough, and made by Sub-Commission No. 12, because the landlord had expended more than £400 on the drainage of the holding during the spring of 1881. The tenant was Patrick Rochefort, and the landlords were R. and H. Doughty. The acreage was 50A. 3R. 14P. statute. The old rent was £39 8s. 6d.; the Government valuation £39; and the new rent has been fixed at £50. The fifth and last increase was made by Sub-Commission No. 8, at Castlerea, county Kilkenny. The tenant was John Fanny, and the landlord Captain Hugh M'Ternan. The acreage amounted to 9A. 2R. 24P. statute. The old rent was £4 10s.; the poor-law valuation £4 5s.; and the new rent was fixed at £5.

Take the directions sketched out by the correspondent of the *Standard*. Consider them by the light of Mr. Porter's words—

who is, you will remember, a responsible Government official— and what, I will ask you, have you left of this impartial tribunal ? Where are the assurances under which, and under which alone, the Bill was passed? There was to be no universal reduction of rents. There is, so far as the Sub-Commissioners have gone, an almost universal reduction, unsupported, so far as I can see, by either principle or reason. There was to be an impartial tribunal ! We have one bound down by the strictest secret instructions, removing all, however, of discretion, the members of it openly threatened by a law officer of the Crown that if they do not proceed in one direction, and in one direction only, they will lose their appointments. I leave the verdict in your hands !

But before I have done with these Sub-Commissions I must say a word upon another point. I ask you to censure them in this resolution for abstaining from stating the principles upon which they act; but I am bound to say, in the very few instances in which they have departed from this rule—when, perhaps, their zeal exceeded their prudence—the reasons which they have announced for arriving at their decisions are not such as are calculated, in my opinion, either to increase or restore our confidence in them. I will refer shortly to a few that occur to me as the most remarkable of them. It has been announced that the rent is not to be fixed according to the value of the land itself, but according to the capability of the occupying tenant to get value out of it. Now, I must say that the extravagance of such a principle is too glaring to require comment. A holding may be of the best description—the land of the richest quality, with every facility for realizing its productiveness. It may be that these very facilities were conferred by the landlord's expenditure; but, according to this new theory, if it be held by a drunkard, a thriftless, idle or slovenly tenant, who, from his own fault, fails to work the holding to profit, the landlord is to get nothing out of it. By this theory a direct premium is held out to all kinds of extravagance, by which it would not be difficult for the fortunate tenant to arrive at the stage of paying no rent at all. Take another instance, and by no means an uncommon one in all parts of the country. The holding small and poor, the family large and soft (as the saying is), how would that be when the tenant applied to have a fair rent fixed ? We had a striking case of such as that before us when I was on the Bessborough Commission at Galway. A witness came forward to represent his own case and that of his neighbours, and stated, as well as I remember, that there were eighteen families living upon fourteen acres of poor land. He did not ground his complaint upon excess of rent; that, I believe, was something nominal ; but he declared that if he held the land for nothing he could not live on it. Now, if we follow this newly announced principle in this case to its logical sequence, it is clear that the landlord, instead of receiving rent, should pay the tenant for occupying his land. We have another announcement not a bit less extraordinary, in the case of a tenant holding a rich bit of meadow land, I think in the vicinity of the city of Limerick. It was proved that the land had been of considerable value from its inherent fertility ; but this went for nothing on the landlord's behalf, because it was proved for the tenant that by taking excellent crops of meadow off it, year after year, without putting a single bit of manure on it, he had entirely exhausted it. The rent was reduced to the value, I believe, to that the tenant had, by his wanton, and, I might almost say, malicious conduct, deteriorated it. I feel that I should only weaken such a case as that by enlarging on it. There are many others, but time will not permit of my referring to them, and I will only, before I leave the subject altogether, allude to one which has been brought under my notice by a letter in the *Standard* of last week, written by a Southern landowner, who appeared to me to state in a plain and simple manner a very pitiable case, and one that I believe will prove, if these decisions go on and remain unreversed, to be typical of many others. He stated that he was a tenant for life on an estate of £4000 per annum, bound by his tenure to let his lands at the full value, without taking any fine. This kind of tenure is common on many properties in the country. His land was let at one-third over Griffith's valuation, which I have never heard named as an extravagant figure. The Sub-Commissioners reduced his rental to £3,000 per annum, or something about our " old friend Griffith." That is very like the rule I read from the *Standard*. For what reason he is thus deprived of a fourth of his income, whether because his tenants were

drunkards or slovenly, or because by bad farming or negligence
they had exhausted their land, he is not to know. All he is to
know is that, whereas once he had £4000 a-year, he has now
got £3000.

I have now shown you as clearly as I can how the Act is
being administered, and I must say for myself that when I
compare Mr. Gladstone's statements and assurances with the
events that are taking place every day under our eyes, I feel
lost in astonishment. I would like to be charitable, and I can
only suppose that Mr. Gladstone must be equally ignorant
of these instructions as of his Solicitor-General's threats. It is
beyond me to believe that he could be capable of passing a measure through Parliament on the assurance that there would be
no universal reduction of rents, and that it should be administered by an impartial tribunal, and then issuing rules making
the universal reduction compulsory, and depriving these admi-
nistrators of all power of being impartial or in the least degree
exercising their judgment on the issues submitted to them. I
should be sorry, as I have said, to believe that he, or, indeed,
any minister, was capabable of such action. But there is no
doubt of this fact, that he will be responsible if, after his attention has been called to what is going on, he sanctions the
continuance of such proceedings, or leaves these reports uncon-
tradicted. This in itself I think shows the importance of our
meeting here to-day. It is not only our interests as Irish
landowners that are involved—the question is much wider,
and must touch either the nation's honour or the nation's
purse.

Now, this brings me to a subject which, although hardly
covered by the resolution which I am in charge of, is one of
such general and deep-felt interest that I must ask your leave
to touch upon it. It is the question of compensation—it has a
twofold aspect. One is both the direct and indirect loss inflicted
upon landowners by the general effect of this legislation upon
the land question. It is one of enormous magnitude, upon
which I hold very strong views, already expressed in my sepa-
rate report on the Bessborough Commission, and which I shall
not be backward in supporting when the time comes for so
doing. To try to do so now would, I feel, without in any

way either advancing or strengthening our case—rather the reverse—waste the time at our disposal, and expose me to the unpleasant ordeal of being called to order. The other aspect is the question of compensation arising out of these decisions; but although I believe that it is one clearly within our present scope, I must say frankly at once that I should regard any formulated claim put forward now as premature, and so damaging to our position. We have no right to assume that the decisions of these Head Commissioners on appeals brought before them will confirm the rulings of the Sub-Commissioners. They may take—I believe they will—a juster view of this, and we have no right to condemn them indirectly by seeking compensation on the assumption that they will not before they are tried. If they confirm these decisions there will, no doubt, be a heavy bill for the Government to meet, with a far higher and stronger claim than ever the Jamaica slave-owners had in support of their demand for compensation. I must apologise for comparing Irish landowners with those who trafficked in the bodies and destinies of men, but in business matters we must reduce them to a mercantile rule or basis. We have on our behalf on this count the instance of Mr. Gladstone's family as the recipients of £63,454 17s. 1d. of the British taxpayers' money as compensation for rights that they surrendered. And have men who bought their property no right to compensation for now being deprived of a part of it? I have no doubt there are some here present who have under the Landed Estates Court purchased property the rents existing on which were guaranteed to them by their title. No man can say that they did wrong in so doing; but more than that, there hardly ever was a sale under that Court that was not published by an advertisement, to the effect that the existing rents on the properties advertised for sale might fairly be raised. Men bought on this inferred guarantee; they bought as a speculation, and they raised their rents on the good faith of the Government advertisement that they had a right to do so. The fact that they had this right is not controverted, but the fact that they did so is one of the causes which has created the present trouble, and tended to produce the Act the results of which we are now discussing. In such cases as this I apprehend there is little doubt that even if brought before the Head

Commission the result will be a loss of income to them. Does a Parliamentary title give them no right to compensation? If it does not, I must say the Incumbered Estates Court Act is not worth the parchment it is written on. But I am not here to-day to defend their action. I am no supporter of rack renting, whatever may be the extent or nature of such legal rights.

When we are dealing with matters of property which involve directly or indirectly the interests, I may say the destinies, of our fellow-men, I am no advocate for the exaction of the "pound of flesh," and more especially when that "pound" is weighed by the standard of an Incumbered Estates Court advertisement. If then they are entitled to compensation, how much stronger is the claim of those whose estates, according to the Bessborough report, are considerately managed, and to whom the credit is due of never having exacted all that they were entitled to exact. Does their forbearance give them no claim?—their time and money spent in promoting their tenants' interests create for them no equity? Are their incomes to be cut down by this system of administering the Land Act without repayment? Are their properties to be rendered valueless by the agitation avowedly permitted—I have Mr. Chamberlain as my authority—to facilitate and secure its passing, and are they to recieve no compensation? I can quote Mr. Gladstone's words bearing directly upon this point, on July 22nd:—"I am determined, as far as I am personally concerned—and I think I can, speaking for friends near me, say that they share in my determination—that in doing our duty to the several classes in Ireland who are immediately affected by the Bill, we shall not forget the duty we owe to the nation at large. If those classes, either or both of them, have a just claim for compensation in consequence of the manner in which their interests will be affected by the Bill, we are bound, as a Parliament, to give them compensation." These are strong words, which may hereafter form the ground-work and manual for our future action. But while appeals are still unheard — while the justice, independence, and impartiality, of the Head-Commissioners remain unjustified before these confiscatory reductions are confirmed, it would, in my opinion, be premature to formulate a claim which we might, with some truth, be informed was only based upon a hypothetical loss.   If the decisions of these Sub-Commissioners are confirmed—if this agitation goes on unchecked, and the country be rendered more uninhabitable than it is, and our properties unsaleable, then, indeed, we shall be in a position to claim the redemption of Mr. Gladstone's promise, and our bill will be a heavy one.   But, as I understand it, the object of this meeting here to-day is to call public attention, both in this country and in England, to the manner in which this Act is being administered, and to record our protest against it.   I can speak at least for myself that such is the reason for my being here—not only in the interests of myself and the class to which I have the honour to belong, but in the interests also of the British taxpayer—to call the attention of those in England, who may have a heavy bill to pay, to how things are going on—to stop, if possible, this reckless confiscation ; but if not successful in that, to prevent those who hereafter may have to defray the cost from having cause to complain that they were not warned of what was coming.   His resolution was in these words:—

" That this meeting protest in the strongest manner against the action of the Assistant-Commissioners, inasmuch as it observes that in determining what is a fair rent, they appear to rest their decisions mainly upon their own cursory inspection of the lands during hurried visits in the depths of winter; that, contrary to the practice of all other courts, they fail to state the grounds of their judgments, thus doing great injustice to parties who may desire to appeal against their decisions; that while it is to be presumed, and has been stated by some of them, that they are guided by certain definite principles, they have abstained from announcing what those principles are, and they proceed as if they were bound to make an indiscriminate reduction of rents.

MR. FRANCIS DAMES-LONGWORTH, Q.C.,

seconded the motion. He said:—

I have to apologize for the paucity of my remarks by
mentioning that it was not until yesterday evening that my
friend Colonel King-Harman requested me to supply the gap
that had unfortunately taken place in the proceedings of
the day in consequence of an accident to one of the members
of Mr. Mulholland's family. But no man in the community,
no matter how humble he may be—no matter how mean his
talents or ability may be—has a right, when called upon, to
refuse to come to the forefront, and to do battle so far as
he can to support the rights of property in this country. It
has been truly remarked that this matter passed altogether
from the ranks of party politics the moment the Land Act
became law.

We are all here united as loyal men to point attention
to matters which are of grave concern and grave consideration, to strengthen if we can, and to support the hands of
the executive Government—to call attention to matters which,
if unredressed, must, as one of the papers this morning said,
lead to chaos and anarchy. We are anxious to show the
Government of the country the points in which we believe
the action of the present land system has been a failure.
The resolution which has been so ably proposed by Mr.
Kavanagh—and indeed, but for the fact that he proposed
it, I would not undertake to second it—contains an indictment against the Sub-Commissioners who are carrying out
the Land Act. It contains an indictment of a three-fold
character against them, or, as we lawyers say, three counts,
and it will be for this meeting to say which of the counts
is the most serious in respect to their conduct. The first
is that they, in administering the duties which have been
imposed on them, have—I will not say wilfully—I wish to
avoid the imputation of motives—but that they have mistaken their mission—a serious count in itself, but I do not
think it is the most serious one. We also indict them that
they in pursuing their inquiries have acted upon evidence

of a most unsatisfactory character. As decisions of all courts of justice should be based upon evidence of a truthful and reliable character, I ask you whether that count is of a serious character or not. Lastly, as the decisions of these Sub-Commissioners are not to be final with regard to the property of this country, I conceive that the third count is the most important, in which we charge that they in their decisions, having made no declarations as to their grounds, have left the suitor who may be desirous to appeal in a most helpless condition, such as no court of justice over the world, or no court of justice in this land at least, has ever done.

I read in the paper this morning a letter from Lord Monck, in which he said the Sub-Commissioners were appointed to perform novel, difficult, and invidious duties. I think I may give them credit for this—that they have performed them in a novel and invidious manner, and I may add that in the performance of these duties they have experienced but little difficulty. The first count against them is that they have mistaken their mission, and that instead of going forth, according to the words of the Act of Parliament, to fix a fair rent, they have gone forth to reduce rents. By the returns we have received we learn that the reductions of rents, up to the 31st of December, have been £4,322 15s. 3d., and the additions have been only £16 2s. 2d. Therefore, I say it appears, on evidence incontrovertible, that they have mistaken their mission.

It is perfectly incredible that for a period which we need not measure back the whole of the tenantry of Ireland have been paying unfair rents, as these decisions would pronounce them to be. It is a startling proposition, which will not commend itself to the good sense of those I have the honour to address. I read of one case, at Erlingford, where the rent was pronounced to be a fair rent as paid to the landlord, but that rent was in the same breath reduced, because of temporary abatements or reductions in bad years, through the indulgence or liberality of the landlord. I have read of a case in which the Sub-Commissioners thought the rent was too low, and then there is put upon the landlord the invidious task of saying

whether he will apply to have the rent raised. I humbly say
that in a case of this kind the landlord should not be asked to
answer that question, and the proper duty of the Sub-Commissioners would be to fix the fair rent, no matter whether the
landlord asked them to do so or not. Well, now, on the second
point—namely, the evidence upon which the Commissioners
proceed—could anything be more startling or unsatisfactory in
the history of judicial proceedings? We know the difficulty
which landlords have in procuring evidence upon questions of
value. We know the difficulty under which landlords labour
in even having leave given to their valuer to enter on the lands
of their tenants. And I believe I am in the hearing of those
who can correct me if I am wrong, that the Commissioners in
Dublin have had to postpone the hearing of a number of cases
because of the intimidation practised on the landlord's valuer
when he went on the lands of the tenants. Well, the Commissioners—they hear the evidence, they adjourn, and the three
gentlemen on some frosty December morning—perhaps when
the lands are flooded, as most low-lying lands are at this season
—go and take a cursory view of the land. It will be an
interesting matter of inquiry, when some of these cases come on
appeal before the Chief Commissioners, what portion of the
lands they have travelled over. I know a gentleman who
followed them with an ordnance map in his hand, and, if I am
not misinformed, the hearing of the appeals will disclose an
extraordinary contradiction to the statement of the Commissioners when they returned into court that they had " carefully
examined the lands." Certainly, the extent of farms valued in
an incredibly short time would lead one to the conclusion that
the information I have received is not very incorrect. With
regard to the legal Commissioner, he knows very little about it.
One of them—I will not give you any name—told me the other
day he knew nothing about land; he was trying to learn something, but as to his deciding whether land was worth 20s. or
30s. an acre the idea was absurd. Well, the other two make
a cursory inspection of the land, and they come back into court,
and in every case they base their decision largely upon the
inspection they have so made. Well, now, I say this giving a
decision upon not only unsworn testimony, not subjected to

cross-examination, but the reasons of which are not even disclosed to the litigant parties—am I right, then, in saying that this is a species of administration of justice unknown in this country; and certainly unparalleled so far as it has gone? When they have come to their decision, could anything be more unsatisfactory than the way in which it is announced? The legal gentleman, who knows not the difference between a Swede and an Aberdeen turnip, gives the decision of the other two Commissioners on a subject with which he is not conversant; he is, in fact, made the official mouthpiece to deliver that judgment, because, if the reasons for the judgment are to be concealed, it is as well to keep a gentleman who does not know the reasons, and cannot explain them, to pronounce the judgment in court. It is like as if the Lord Chief Justice in the Queen's Bench, after having heard an elaborate argument on a nice and intricate point of law, were to say to one of the other officers of the court, "You deliver the judgment in this case, and give just as much of the reasons for it as you know yourself." It was most unsatisfactory to have decisions based upon evidence unknown, and reasons that were not disclosed.

I have every respect for the public courts of my country, but, as regards these mushroom courts, which spring up in a night, governed by no intelligible principle—I speak not against individuals, but the courts themselves, judged by the decisions they have made—I can speak without much hesitation or reserve. There are other directions in which the decisions of these courts have gone hardly against the landlords, and the result of which has been to largely increase the business of these courts. I should say, as between man and man, that if I am to be mulcted in costs by my tenant for not charging a fair rent, it would be only fair, before he came into court, to ask the court to fix a fair rent, that he should approach me, and see if I will meet him in a conciliatory spirit. Take an estate of five hundred tenants for instance—and there are many such in Ireland—by the time they all come into court, if the costs of both parties are to fall on the landlord—and we may estimate the costs in each case would not be less than £10—that would make a tax upon the landlord of £5000 in addition to the loss of his income. I believe, from some recent cases I have seen in the paper, the action of the Sub-Commissioners in this respect is being rather amended, and I commend these observations to their consideration if they think them worthy of it.

Now I have been warned that the time is short, and, therefore, I have concentrated my observations upon what I am more familiar with—the ordinary fair procedure of a court of justice so called. This is a court constituted to decide enormous rights; it has been deciding enormous rights. It is a court which is bringing misery and ruin to the homes of many a happy family. It is a court which, where the rent has been paid, undisturbed for forty, or fifty, or sixty years—*prima facie* reason why it should not be reduced—proceeds, without giving any reasons, to reduce it. I, therefore, with Mr. Kavanagh, call upon you unanimously to pass this resolution which I have so feebly seconded. I thank you very much for the hearing you have given me.

The resolution was passed.

The EARL of WESTMEATH

proposed the next resolution :—

" That, inasmuch as the Land Act has been administered by the Assistant-Commissioners in a manner not contemplated by Parliament, this meeting is of opinion that the appeals from their decisions should be heard by the Chief Commissioners without further delay ; that, pending such appeals, their further action should be stayed ; and that, if such appeals should result in sanctioning the decisions of the Assistant-Commissioners, it would be incumbent on the Legislature to provide compensation for those landowners and others whose property would be thereby unjustly diminished."

He said :—

My Lord Duke, my Lords and Gentlemen — The fifth resolution has been given to me to put forward for your consideration. I do so with much reluctance and diffidence. With reluctance, because I know that in this vast and influential assembly there are men who could give expression to the motion in far better terms than I can ; and with diffidence, because I am now, for the first time in my life, addressing such an influential assembly, and on such a momentous subject.

But, my Lords and Gentlemen, the time has now come, as it has been observed here to-day, when it behoves every man, notwithstanding what his station in this country may be, to speak out in defence of his property and rights. We are not assembled here to cavil at the Land Act, which has now become law, but to express our surprise and consternation at the ruthless manner in which its provisions are being administered through the length and breadth of the land—a way, I venture to say, not contemplated by the majority of the party under whose auspices it became law. I venture to say, without fear of contradiction, that this Act is not carried out in the spirit contemplated by Parliament, according to the statement of leading politicians, and according to the report of the Bessborough Commission, by whom no such sweeping reductions were expected. The Assistant-Commissioners have given their decisions on concealed principles, responsible to no one, but subject to correction on appeal. It is stated the Chief Commissioners intend to hear appeals shortly. Now we, the representatives of that class who consider themselves injured, desire it to be clearly understood by the public and by Parliament, that we demand an immediate expounding of the principles upon which the Act is being administered, and that we should know without delay whether what we consider as extreme and unfair decisions meet with the approval of the Chief Commissioners. If the result of the appeals should go to prove that the Assistant-Commissioners have given, to say the least, extreme decisions, the landlord class will, to some extent, be relieved from the conviction that whatever the intention of the promoters of the Act, its operations will be to many ruin. If, on the other hand, the Chief Commissioners refuse to divulge the principles upon which they believe the Act should be administered, or to announce such principles as will justify them in upholding the decisions of the Assistant-Commissioners, then the question of how Parliament is to compensate those who, contrary to the expressed opinions of several of the promoters of the Act, have been sacrificed to what some who now try to defend its operations say was necessary for the public welfare, as to how, and to what extent, that compensation should be granted, will entirely depend on the result of the appeals.

My Lords and Gentlemen, in conclusion, I will say no more, after the brilliant oratory which we have heard to-day. But there is one who, I understand, will come after me, who will be able fully to enter into this resolution, and who will make up for my defects.

COLONEL KING-HARMAN,

who was greeted with loud applause on coming forward, said—

My Lord Duke, my Lords and Gentlemen—In seconding the resolution which has been put into my hands, I am impressed with the opinion that, important as the previous resolutions have been, and worthy as they have been of being received with acclamation by you, this fifth resolution is more important than all. Because time presses—we cannot wait.

For two or three years past the Irish landed gentry have had many and grievous burdens to bear. Our country suffered under privations, famine and sore distress. The Irish landlords, to their credit be it said, came forward and assisted the distress. They did not press for their rents in these hard times. They went without money; they borrowed far and wide to relieve the distress at hand. I have heard it stated, indeed I have been taunted with it myself, that we were too lavish, too indiscriminate in our aid, and that we gave relief where distress was only simulated. Well, we may have, but that is not a thing to be ashamed of. What has been our reward? The hands that were raised to us in supplication, and that we once thought would have turned to us in thankfulness, are turned bitterly against us. Instead of *cead mille failthe* we have the curse and the scowl; and the outcome of this ingratitude is what? A Bill to relieve and help—not the poor and distressed—but those who, by our forbearance, emerged safely from a period of distress, and who have had the finest harvest that has been known in the memory of man, and who are well able to pay their rents —far better, as the Prime Minister himself has said, than the tenant-farmers of England and Scotland.

Now, to carry out this Bill, a host of Assistant-Commis-sioners, into whose merits I will not go, as they have been several times described to you, have been let loose over the land, and wherever they have gone the same extraordinary spectacle has been witnessed, and the same extraordinary de-cisions have been heard. Rents which have been freely, honestly, and easily paid for half a century have, without rhyme or reason, and against rhyme and reason, been cut down. Where are the Chief Commissioners, in whose integ-rity, and skill, and ability the English Parliament put their trust, and whose names the people of Ireland received with a certain amount of confidence. What have they been doing for the last two months while these cases were being heard, that everybody knew perfectly well could only end in one way, while the fate of thousands has been trembling in the balance, and while the fortunes of hundreds have been tossed to the winds by the decisions in this country?

This resolution that I am seconding calls upon you to de-mand that appeals against these miserable decisions should be heard without delay; and more, that, pending the hearing of these appeals, the proceedings of the Sub-Commissioners should be stayed. What would be the use of the Head Commissioners hearing one appeal which would take the court a-week, while a dozen roving Commissioners are going over the country giving ten or twelve decisions, and valuing ten or twelve farms a-day —as a gentleman wrote to me to-day, valuing two farms between a quarter past four o'clock and thirty-five minutes past four o'clock on a December evening—valuing farms as had been done by one of the Sub-Commissioners in a western district lately, who, when called upon to give an opinion of the value of a particular field, thrust his stick into the ground, after the manner of a cheese-taster, smelt it, and said "15s. an acre." I say that we have a right to call upon her Majesty's Government to stay these tasting and smelling examinations until those in whose experience or whose knowledge and wisdom we may have some confidence have had time to overhaul the decisions pre-viously given.

It must be perfectly clear to the meeting, if it is not per-fectly clear to every man's individual intelligence before, that the British Parliament would never have passed the Land Bill if it had not been clearly understood that the whole of its administration was to be entrusted to the management of those three gentlemen whose names were approved by Parliament. At the time the Bill was going through the House of Commons a committee of Irish gentlemen was sitting in London, trying to move or get moved amendments which we thought from our intimate knowledge of the country might be useful. And I ventured to suggest that the appointment of these Sub-Commissioners should not rest with the Government or with the Lord Lieutenant, but with the Chief Commissioners themselves. My reasons were these. I considered in the first place that the Chief Commissioners, being men of large and varied experience, would know thoroughly the claims and qualifications of the men to whom they were giving the offices of assistants; and further, I thought it was clear that the honour of the Chief Commissioners would be bound up in the efficiency of the Assistant-Commissioners, and if the Chief Commissioners had their appointment they would be responsible for their misdemeanours, and mistakes and errors. But as it is now they can turn round and say, "We know nothing of these men; they were appointed by the Government, and we are not responsible for their mistakes." But I say now, make them responsible at once by forcing them to hear appeals. Let there be no further delay. Delay is cruel—it is not only cruel to the landlord, but cruel to the unfortunate tenant, because every one of those cases decided brings hundreds more into court; every one of these decisions of injustice against the landlord raises higher the hopes of the peasantry; and every decision of that kind diminishes the feeling of honesty and honour in the minds of those in whose breasts there is still left some honour and honesty. Further than that, I say it is cruel, because the majority of these decisions must be upset. It is impossible that they can be otherwise, because the decisions of one court are exactly contrary to the decisions of another court; and where you have half a dozen decisions in different courts differing as far as possible, it must be perfectly clear that if the decisions of one court be right, the decisions of the other five must be wrong; and if the appeals against the decisions be sustained—as they must be—think of the bitter pang of disappointment which the unfortunate tenant must feel when, thinking he had got his rent reduced, and was going to get his holding at far below its proper value, and had been rejoicing, and exulting, and revelling in the result of the case; that when he comes before the Chief Commissioners his hopes are crushed, and so, instead of being a messenger of peace to him, it will be a message of bitterness and sorrow. The Land League then outside, point at him, and say, "Aha! didn't we tell you so? Didn't we tell you there would be no use in going into the Land Court?" This is how the Government sends peace on earth, goodwill towards men at this happy Christmas time. This is how the people will be taught to reverence the decisions of the law, and the lawyers and experts who have been sent to administer it.

I will touch one small point before I conclude as to the operations of the Assistant-Commissioners. A friend of mine—a valuator of great experience—was giving his evidence the other day in one of the courts, and his evidence was, that he valued the farm let at £52 a-year by the landlord at £45 a-year, but he stated that the farm had been, chiefly through the improvements made by the landlord, worth considerably more, and he considered that the Assistant-Commissioners should put on a larger rent than the value put on the farm at the present day as compensation for deterioration of the most pronounced description committed by the tenant, and further, that he believed that if the same tenant remained in the farm for fifteen years more, at the end of that time the farm, instead of being worth £45, would not be worth £20. The Assistant-Commissioners distinctly stated that they had no power to take the question of deterioration into consideration at all. Now, it is within my recollection that when the Bill was passing through the House of Commons the question of deterioration was two or three times brought under the attention of the Government, and strongly urged on them, and the Minister in charge of the Bill invariably said that it was a point which the Commissioners and the Sub-Commissioners would undoubtedly take cognizance of. Here you have the Assistant-Commissioners repudiating the authority with which they were clothed, and in two other

cases you have the legal Commissioners giving decisions com-
pelling the landlord to pay county cess, in distinct opposition to
the ruling of Lord Justice Christian and others in a celebrated
case—showing, I think, very conclusively, that while agricultural experts are not quite so qualified or experienced in the
value of land as they might be, the legal Commissioners are not
completely immaculate as regards their knowledge of law. The
hour is late, and I had not intended to inflict a long speech
upon you; and I may further say if I had intended I would
have been unable to do so, because every speaker before me has
taken a plum out of my pudding, and has left me nothing but
dry matter to deal with.

I therefore conclude by urging strongly upon you the
necessity of passing this resolution with acclamation; but
before sitting down I would just turn to one remark that
fell from Mr. Mahony in his brilliant speech. He said that
in a certain event one course only was open—that the course
of sedition was not open to us—and he represented that course
as, practically speaking, emigration on a large scale of the
loyal classes from Ireland. I think there is another course
which I commend to your notice—a course which should have
been taken by us long ago, and which should be taken by us
now, and which this meeting makes me hope may still be
taken, and that course is *united action*. We have been beaten
in detail, and struck down one by one while the others looked
on. In many parts of Ireland it seemed to be a race with the
landlords who should give in quickest. Let it now be with us
a point of honour who shall stand stoutest, shoulder to shoulder.
Who have we been beaten by ? Has it been by men of unex-
ampled talent and great experience ? Nothing of the kind.
We, the educated class, have been struck down by men of
little education ; we, the men whose fathers showed no craven
front in former days, are cowed before a despicable foe. Let
this be no longer the case. Stand together with determination
and fixity of purpose; let our watchword be " no surrender,"
and above all, " fatherland."

The resolution was then passed with acclamation.

MR. R. U. PENROSE FITZGERALD,

who was received with applause, said—

My Lord Duke, my Lords and Gentlemen—the late hour at which we have arrived enables me to state that I shall let you off with five-sixths of what I was going to say; and also for the further reason to which Colonel King-Harman has referred—that all I had intended to say has been already said by those who have preceded me. A resolution has been intrusted to me to propose, and I shall now read it to you—

"That an humble petition to Her Most Gracious Majesty the Queen, embodying the views of this meeting, be signed by those present; that the Executive Committee be directed to adopt measures so as to enable others not now present to append their signatures; and that his Grace the Duke of Abercorn be requested to transmit the same to the Secretary of State, to be laid before her Majesty."

In proposing that resolution to you, I only ask you to exercise a constitutional right in a constitutional country. I am asking you to do it in a country where up to now I have thought that Constitution as near perfect as it could possibly be; but in the last two or three years those of us who have lived in this country have seen justice in contempt and law in abeyance, and we have seen freedom murdered by a semi-lawful lawlessness, and seen liberty mutilated by mob law. Therefore I ask you to adopt this resolution, and to do this constitutional thing in a constitutional way. It is unnecessary for me to detain you with any criticism of the mode in which this Act is being administered.

I wish to point out to you one or two things in connexion with these Sub-Commissioners, whose proceedings have been tolerably well sifted here to-day. Let me mention this: First, we have the Legal Commissioners. Of them I know very little except that, so far as I do know them, it would be perfectly true that the most of them could tell you how many lines of engrossment could be put on a parchment rather than the number of animals that could be fed on an acre. Then we have another—a relation of the secretary of the local Land League, if not exactly in his own district, certainly in a district not far from it. He gives his decision, and goes home to rest among his friends. I need not tell you what his bias is likely to be. Then we have a third—a man who in most cases is a professor taken from some Government seminary in the country. And these are the people we are to have our estates valued by. I need not detain you further on this subject.

Colonel King-Harman referred to the county cess. There is something more behind what he mentioned to you. It is the tax out of which comes the damages for malicious injuries; and if the tax be now sought to be put on the landlords, and taken off the tenants, why in future, when malicious injury is committed, unless the landlords take to burning their tenants' stacks, the landlords themselves will have their own stacks burned, and will be called upon to pay for it.

LORD DE FREYNE

seconded the resolution. He said—

I have great pleasure in seconding the resolution which has been so ably proposed, and which needs no words of mine to recommend it.

The resolution was adopted.

The EARL OF BELMORE.

My Lords and Gentlemen, I have been asked to move the next resolution, and I do so with pleasure. It is as follows:—

"That copies of the foregoing resolutions be forwarded by the chairman to His Excellency the Lord Lieutenant and the Prime Minister, and that this meeting be now adjourned to a day to be hereafter fixed by the Executive Committee, by whom at least ten days' notice shall be given of the day on which such adjourned meeting shall be held."

This is a resolution which, if I may venture to use the expression, gives motive power to the other resolutions that have gone before it. In the speeches that we have all listened to with so much pleasure, our attenton has been called to the various points in the resolutions in an able and exhaustive manner, and it will not, therefore, be necessary for me to do more than to notice them in a very cursory way. Why is it that we are here to-day ? Why is it that this great and closely-packed meeting is here to-day ? It is because we feel that we are brought face to face with a great national calamity. It is not merely because we feel that our own class, the class that owns the land in Ireland, is menaced, but also that the vital interests of those who are interested in land, the labourers and those who have to depend upon the landlord class, are menaced. And depend upon it if this class should be swept away other classes will suffer. If you destroy capital invested in land, it will be felt that capital otherwise invested will not be very secure, for capital, as we all know, is a very shy bird indeed.

The passing of the Land Act through Parliament is sufficiently close for us all to remember what then occurred. We were distinctly assured by the Prime Minister, the Lord Chancellor, and others, that the average value of property would not be depreciated; on the contrary, it was affirmed that, owing to the greater security the Act would give for the payment of rents judicially fixed, it would be increased. But what do we now see ? We see property in the Landed Estates Court almost absolutely unsaleable, and we see an average reduction of incomes from land of 25 per cent. Lord Monck seems to think that 25 per cent. reduction is not very much to be grumbled at. 25 per cent. of an average means a very much larger reduction in a great many cases : it means a reduction in many instances below Griffith's valuation. We have heard *ad nauseam* what Griffith's valuation is. We know that it is a mere rating valuation, and that in various districts varying sums should be added to arrive at a fair rent. It is not my intention to say much about the Assistant-Commissioners. It is not a pleasant thing to deal in personalities, and I do not care to do it. But I must remind you that in all the discussions in Parliament on the question of fair rent we were always assured that the rents would be fixed by the Head Commissioners themselves. It was not known at that time what the exact duties of the Assistant-Commissioners would be, for they were not clearly defined. What do we find now ? We find that the Head Commissioners have devolved upon the Assistant-Commissioners the whole of the duty in the first instance of fixing the rent. The Head Commissioners themselves were asked, I believe, to try a few test cases, in order to give the public some idea of what the standard should be. They declined to do so, and left the matter to be dealt with by the Sub-Commissioners. Mr. Mulholland, who, I am sorry, is prevented from being with us to-day, in a speech he made in the House of Commons with reference to the Sub-Commissioners, said that after all they could only be valuators, whereupon Mr. Gladstone informed him that the Assistant-Commissioners would not be valuators. We now see that they are valuators. And how do they arrive at a definition of a fair rent? In general terms, they go in for a reduction of rent. Professor Baldwin has told us that they have some plan by which they arrived at a fair rent, but what that plan is he has not informed us. They appear to forget that the rent of the man who is owner of the land is a preferential charge upon it. They take into account the tenant's interest in the land, the expense of the management, and, if possible, the extent of the family; and, after deducting all expenses from what they believe the land produces, they say what is left is the landlord's rent. I maintain that that is an entirely erroneous and false plan on which to proceed.

We are all agreed that we are not here to pick holes in the Act itself. For my own part I may say that I never concealed my opinion that I thought the principle of the Land Court an erroneous principle. I do not see how you are to ascertain the value of anything unless by seeing what it will bring in the open market. We have passed a resolution calling upon the Head Commissioners to hear appeals at once, and to suspend the action of the Sub-Commissioners until they have done so. There is one very unanswerable reason for that resolution. The actual money value of the reductions made in the rentals of all the estates from which tenants have come into court is, according to the returns we have heard, a little over £4000; and if compensation is to be provided, it will not amount to a very large sum.

It seems to me that compensation may be based on two grounds—one ground is the actual value of the land—what would be a fair rent for it in the open market. Then there is another ground, and that is the altered position which the working of this Act has given to the landlords. An election has lately taken place in the county of Derry, and the Solicitor-General made a great many speeches at that election, with most of which I disagree. But he said one thing that I think is very true. He said, " The freehold in point of fact has passed to the tenant." I did not see the speech, but I saw a letter written by Sir Frederick Heygate upon that portion of it. Surely that alone is a ground for granting compensation. Then again, if the land is not to rise in value in the hands of the landlord, but to decrease for the next fifteen years, that also would be a good ground for compensation. I will not detain you any longer, and I therefore beg to move the resolution.

COLONEL FFOLLIOTT.

At this very late hour at which it is my privilege to address you, I intend to do little more than second the resolution. Very little—nothing, I may say—remains for me to state but this : I do say from the bottom of my heart that I congratulate your Grace and this great meeting upon the success which has attended our proceedings. Probably never in the life of any one of us—certainly not in my own life—has there been held a meeting of such paramount importance as this. Some of us may have feared that the subject might not be treated in a manner worthy of it ; but such fears have not been realized. There is not one man in this room who did not realize that the importance of this meeting was far beyond all party politics, and went down to the very foundations of civilization and liberty. We have met here men of all shades of politics, and we have heard not a word of party difference. We knew we were dealing with a matter of vast importance—the sacredness of private property —and once the sacredness of private property is destroyed, there is an end to civilization.

Now, your Grace, when I speak of property, I do not allude to the property of the rich alone. The property of the poor man is as sacred to my eyes as the property of the rich man. The property of the poor Irish tenant—a class of people among whom I have lived all my life—the property of the poor Irish tenantry is as dear to me as my own. What I say is this, your

Grace, touch one class of private property, and you can never consider that any other class is safe. But we shall be told, probably, to-morrow morning by some of the papers, that landed property is totally different from all other kinds of property. I do not deny that, but it so happens that property in land has been taken under the special guardianship of the British Government. It has been taken specially under the protection of the British Government in the way in which any other kind of property is taken under its protection. You remember how, through the Incumbered Estates Court, the British Government undertook to be salesmasters of private property, and put forward splendid catching advertisements, as any salesmaster might do setting forth a rental, not at Griffith's valuation, but setting forth the letting value of the land, and adding in some cases— "At the falling in of a lease the rental of this property may be doubled." The British Government, acting as the salesmaster, did not say to those who purchased, "We offer you a certain rental, which never can be made less or greater." Still less did they sell with a condition added that this rental cannot be increased, but it may probably be reduced. If they had done that, probably not one purchaser would be found in the Landed Estates Court. What did happen? Why not only wealthy landlords, who wanted a bit of land that lay into their estates, but shopkeepers, who had accumulated money in neighbouring towns, went into the court and gave enormous prices for land to make provision for their families. Purchases at enormous prices were then made, and when the rentals are now being reduced there is an absolute and just claim for compensation. It seems to me impossible to deny that for one moment. It cannot be denied by any man of honour. It has been a principle always —in every civilized country—that what a man has inherited or what he has bought with his money is his absolute property, and cannot be taken from him without compensating him for it. The individual instance in which another kind of property was confiscated has been already referred to—the case of the slave-holders. It was very right to take away their property. I am not going to say that it is not just as right to take away the right of property in land from us: perhaps it is; but there is some little difference in the two cases. The slaves were brought from their native country under every circumstance of barbarity and horror that could possibly be imagined, and in defiance of every law human and divine ; and when the British Government deprived the owners of those slaves of their property they paid them for the loss. Possibly there are persons in high positions in England who, no doubt, lecture us from a very high moral position upon the enormity of being Irish landlords and taking anything in the shape of rents, who have been enriched from the money compensation paid for those slaves. I think we have a right to see that men are not condemned to utter poverty for no other crime than that they had relied on the faith of the British Government.

It is terrible to think that old people should be deprived of their all, and that young people should be deprived of their hopes of life for no fault of theirs. Is it too much to say *quousque tandem*—are we to go on enduring and seeing these horrors committed ? I think we are entitled to know what is to be the mode and the measure of chastisement which is about to be inflicted upon us, of whom the Prime Minister has said that we have been tried and had been acquitted. We have been called the garrison of this country, and some approve of our holding that position, and hope that we will remain so. Well, we are a garrison, no doubt, but this is not the only country that requires a garrison. Does not every civilized, well-ordered country require a garrison of well-disposed, honest, right-minded men ? There was no civilized country that could possibly exist without such. Then, why are we twitted by so many with being "the garrison" in this country ? The reason is, that the garrison is small, that our sentry duties are too numerous, and our fatigue duties too heavy. That is the reason we are spoken of as a little garrison with contempt. Yes, we are a small garrison ; but I hope we shall do our duty while we are here. Why is it that the garrison is not larger ? I could answer that question, but it would involve a matter of politics, and I will therefore refrain. The garrison might be larger—three or four times larger—and the aim of all good statesmen should be, not to depress honest, well-disposed, law-abiding men. If they are small in number do not for that reason treat them with contempt or turn them out of the country altogether. If they are too small, he would say to the Government, rather " endeavour to make them larger —do not depress the orderly and well-disposed men upon whom you depend—do not encourage those who would destroy the garrison altogether."—Those issues are not in our hands, but I rejoice to say that going from this meeting we can all think that if our present rulers are determined that this little garrison of law-abiding and moral men—and I speak of no one religion or class, but all Roman Catholics and Protestants, tenants and landlords, shopkeepers, and merchants, all honest men of whatever class or creed—if the Government are determined to depress or destroy us they cannot now, thank God, do so without having received a dignified and solemn protest from this meeting.

SIR GEORGE COLTHURST.

My Lord Duke and Gentlemen, I have had intrusted to my hands what to me is a most pleasing task. I have been asked to convey to your Grace the warmest and most sincere thanks of this great meeting for your able and judicious conduct in the chair. And now, gentlemen, late as it is, I hope you will excuse my pointing out to you that there are two ways of giving thanks. You can cheer, and you can go away and forget all about it ; but, if you want to make the thank-offering really worthy of you who give, and worthy of him who receives, you must take a lesson from this meeting. We have met here to-day from all parts of Ireland—north, south, east, and west—and cannot we, the gentlemen of Ireland, take a lesson from our opponents and organize and combine. We are having hard times just now : our opponents, aye and our candid friends, accuse us of apathy and want of energy—even of cowardice. Gentlemen, let your answer to that be in deeds and not in words.

Even now, if at the eleventh hour the landlords of Ireland could join in one common bond of union ; if ignoring all personal interests, postponing, or perhaps surrendering their favourite amusements, they would work for the welfare— aye the very existence of the class to which they belong— at all events, if we are to pass away, if our name is to be no more known in the land, no man could shame us by saying that we behaved like cowards. You may easily cavil at the advice I give, because of the youth and inexperience of the speaker; but forgive me for urging on you at this dark moment the necessity of working for yourselves. Cannot you join those organizations; cannot you try to help yourselves, instead of calling out to others? And I believe from the bottom of my heart, if you are united, we have a chance of winning the battle which is waged against us; but, if divided, there is nothing left but to fall.

LORD RATHDONNELL.

I have great pleasure in seconding this resolution, and I only hope that the voice of this meeting will sound through the length and breadth of the land, and that the words spoken here may really and truly bring home to the British public the determination of the landlords of Ireland that they are not going to be put down by any Government without making a struggle for their rigths.

The motion was passed with acclamation.

The EARL of DONOUGHMORE called for three cheers for the DUKE of ABERCORN.

The call was right heartily responded to, the entire audience rising, and cheering most enthusiastically for several minutes. When silence had been restored—

THE DUKE OF ABERCORN

spoke as follows:—

My Lords and Gentlemen, allow me to return you my grateful thanks for the honour you have done me, and for the favourable view you have been pleased to take of my poor services in the Chair. I am conscious myself that I hardly deserve that approval, but I hold that every man in the present distracted state of the country is bound to do whatever in him lies for the protection of the rights of property and the maintenance of law and order. In doing this he is doing no more than he is bound in duty to do. Before sitting down I would again beg to return you my most grateful thanks for the kind manner in which you have supported me to-day in the Chair, and for the way the meeting has united to carry out our proceedings to a successful and useful issue.

As the proceedings of the meeting terminated, the powerful tones of the organ were heard in the music of the National Anthem, which was sung by the audience, standing.

THE following is the petition referred to in the proceedings, and which was signed in the hall by a large number of those attending :—

"PETITION

" TO HER MOST GRACIOUS MAJESTY THE QUEEN.

" The Humble Petition of the undersigned Landowners and others interested in the Land in Ireland—

" HUMBLY SHEWETH,

" That we, while expressing our unalterable attachment and devotion to your Majesty and to the Constitution of the realm, and our readiness, as loyal subjects, to submit to the provisions of the Land Law (Ireland) Act, observe with alarm that that measure is being at present administered in a manner at variance with the pledge given by its promoters, that it would not diminish the value or disturb the foundations of property, and contrary to the assurances on the faith of which Parliament was advised not to provide compensation.

"That while we are convinced that the position, antecedents, experience, and status of the Assistant-Commissioners should be such as to insure the impartial and judicial exercise of their functions, and to command the confidence of suitors and of the public ; we respectfully represent to your Majesty that, in many of the appointments by which these offices have been filled the above considerations appear to have been overlooked.

" That we most respectfully pray your Majesty's gracious attention to the action of the Assistant-Commissioners, inasmuch as we observe that in determining what is a fair rent they appear to rest their decisions mainly upon their own cursory inspection of the lands, during hurried visits in the depths of winter ; that, contrary to the practice of all other courts, they fail to state the grounds of their judgments, thus doing great injustice to parties who may desire to appeal against their decisions; that, while it is presumed, and has been stated by some of them, that they are guided by certain definite principles, they have abstained from announcing what those principles are, and they proceed as if they were bound to make an indiscriminate reduction of rents.

"That we respectfully represent to your Majesty that, owing to the aforesaid unexpected reduction of rents, many landowners in Ireland are threatened with sudden and immediate ruin ; while the security of mortgagees, incumbrancers, and others depending for their income upon landed property, is seriously affected, and in some cases entirely destroyed.

" We therefore humbly beseech your Majesty to take such steps, in conjunction with your Majesty's responsible advisers, as may relieve your petitioners from the calamity with which they are menaced.

"And your Majesty's petitioners, as in duty bound, will ever pray."

www.ingramcontent.com/pod-product-compliance
Lightning Source LLC
Chambersburg PA
CBHW021629270326
41931CB00008B/944